# Hope for Your Marriage

## Harmony for Your Home

MW00824655

**In Partnership with Joe and Michelle Williams**

**ALL RIGHTS RESERVED**

For information on the Marriage 911 ministry, visit our website: www.Marriage911Godsway.com.

No part of this material may be reproduced or photocopied, except as provided by USA copyright law.

All Scripture quotations are taken from HOLY BIBLE, NEW INTERNATIONAL VERSION. Copyright 1973, 1978, 1984 by International Bible Society. Used by permission of Zondervan Publishing House. All rights reserved.

The "NIV" and "New International Version" trademarks are registered in the United States Patent and Trademark Office by International Bible Society. Use of either trademark requires the permission of International Bible Society.

Originally written in 1997 as *Reconciling God's Way*, by Joe and Michelle Williams. Revised and renamed *Marriage 911: First Response* in 2007 by National Institute of Marriage, 412-335-5882, and the International Center for Reconciling God's Way www.Marriage911Godsway.com, 209-581-2789.

Use of *Marriage 911: First Response* name and logo with permission only.

Copyright © 2015 Joe and Michelle Williams
All rights reserved.
ISBN: 978-1-941733-51-6

Published by EA Books Publishing,
a division of Living Parables of Central Florida, Inc. a 501c3
eabooksonline.com

# WELCOME FROM NATIONAL INSTITUTE OF MARRIAGE
www.nationalmarriage.com

Thank you for your willingness and commitment to walk alongside someone who genuinely needs support, encouragement, and accountability in the midst of a marital challenge. Our hearts and prayers are with you both. We now share a common purpose with you; for we, too, come alongside people in marital crises every day. Our team has a wide variety of training and experience, but are all dedicated to one single passion: great relationships. For us, few things in life are more important than helping people experience the kind of fulfilling, meaningful relationships that the Lord desires for them to have. We believe every marriage is worth saving, and every couple can experience the promise of a great marriage. In fact, we believe that the relationships of those who follow Christ should be so extraordinary, that those around them are inspired to develop great relationships with God, self, and others as well.

All of that may sound impossible to you right now, and perhaps you feel as if you need a miracle! At our offices in Branson, Missouri and Rome, Georgia we run the equivalent of a Marriage Emergency Room. We have worked with thousands of couples that everybody had given up on including the couples themselves. The only requirement we have in order to work with them is a "yes" answer to this question:"If God were to work a miracle in your marriage, and the miracle could be the magnitude of the parting of the Red Sea, would you accept it?" That's it. All they have to do is be willing to receive what God may provide for them, even if they may think it impossible. Oh, and by the way, we define a miracle as a marriage with which both people are thrilled ...nothing more, nothing less!

The exciting news is that we witness God doing those types of miracles every single week. Our Lord is alive and well, is passionate about great relationships, and will not withhold Himself from an open and willing heart.

It is our joy and privilege, in partnership with Joe and Michelle Williams, to present this powerful program to you today. Originally written by the Williams in 1997, these books are a newly revised and updated collaboration between our two ministries. We have enthusiastically joined forces, working together more effectively than either ministry could alone. Therefore, the word "we" will refer to statements from all of us, unless otherwise noted.

This program may be all that is needed to open the door for your friend in crisis to experience a life-changing miracle personally and relationally, or it may be just the beginning. Either way, we appreciate your willingness to partner with us and the Williams, and be used as one of God's instruments on this journey. You may even get to witness a miracle! Our entire team at this very moment is standing with you in spirit and in prayer. May God richly bless you for your faithfulness, care, and sacrifice.

Dr. Robert S. Paul and Mark Pyatt
Co-Presidents, National Institute of Marriage

## Introduction

Our names are Joe and Michelle Williams, and we are the Directors and co-founders of the International Center for Reconciling God's Way, Inc. in Modesto, California. We have served in this ministry since 1990. Because we have both experienced divorce in our past before becoming Christians, and separation in our own marriage as Christians, we understand the pain of marriages in crisis. We want to help couples avoid the same mistakes we made. That is why we originally wrote the workbook and support partner handbook that have now been updated and revised in partnership with the National Institute of Marriage. If you have prayerfully agreed to be a support partner for someone going through the Marriage 911: First Response workbook, this handbook will give you some of the tools you will need during your twelve-week commitment.

**Our workbook is both for couples who feel that their marriage needs strengthening and for those who are separated.** The workbook is designed to be completed individually over a twelve-week period, rather than with the spouse. Your commitment and role as a support partner is to meet weekly with the person going through the workbook in order to help them* be accountable for answering the chapter discussion questions, and to pray for them. Don't become their "marriage counselor" unless you are licensed or equipped to do so. We say that for your sake as well as theirs.

**The commitment you are making will be an important factor in  the reconciliation process, so we encourage you to follow the guidelines in this handbook to better allow God to work during the process.** Those of us with a heart for helping couples stay married can easily slip into a "rescue mode" when assisting people in a marriage crisis. We can then find ourselves experiencing burnout when situations escalate or the relationship isn't healing as we think it should. It is our prayer that you will have a joyful experience as you watch God work in the life of the person you are supporting.

Please fill out and mail back the questionnaire we have provided as soon as you can, or you can also go to the nationalmarriage.com website and fill out a brief on-line form in the Marriage 911: First Response section. We all want to pray for you and the person you are supporting. You will also find useful information and resources on their website to help you be successful. Please call the National Institute of Marriage if you have questions or if you would like to order a workbook of your own, at (417) 335-5882.

May God richly bless you as you support the ministry of reconciliation!


Joe Williams
Michelle Williams
Modesto, California

# Contents

## SUPPORT PARTNER GUIDELINES

### I. WHERE'S YOUR FOCUS?

pg. 2    1. Unmet Needs: Do You Expect Your Spouse To Meet All Your Needs?

pg. 5    2. Selfless Behavior: Are You Playing God By Trying to Meet All Your Spouse's Needs?

pg. 8    3. Caring for Self: Are You Exhausted and Feeling Hopeless?

pg. 12    4. Valuing Differences: Do You Want the Freedom to Be Who You Are?

### II. WHERE'S YOUR HEART?

pg. 20    5. Secret Motives: Do You Really Want to Reconcile?

pg. 23    6. Secret Anger: Understand Your Anger...Revolutionize Your Marriage!

pg. 28    7. Secret Lies: Honesty Is At The Core Of True Intimacy

pg. 32    8. Secret Fears: What Keeps You From Being Real With Your Mate?

### III. WHERE'S YOUR HOPE?

pg. 36    9. Know How To Recognize Hope: Bad Habits Are Hard To Break

pg. 39    10. Know What To Avoid: God's Timing Is Not Always Ours

pg. 42    11. Know Who's On Your Team: Turn Opposition Into Optimism

pg. 46    12. Know When To "Go Forth": Whatever The Outcome, Use It For Good

# SUPPORT PARTNER GUIDELINES

- **You must have a personal relationship with Jesus Christ, attend church regularly, and commit to faithfully pray for this couple's marriage.**

- **If you are married, your own marriage should not be in crisis.** Everyone's marriage needs tuning up now and then, and we encourage you to join the person you are supporting by purchasing your own workbook and going through the lessons. If your own marriage is in crisis, however, we recommend that you turn down the request to be a support partner, and get help for your own relationship first.

- **Meet separately rather than as couples (i.e., men together, women together).** In fact, it is generally advisable to avoid being the support partner to the spouse of someone that your own husband/wife is supporting. This is a very important element in avoiding unfortunate, and often unforeseen, situations for everyone involved. We have had support couples get into heated arguments themselves due to differences of opinions regarding the couple in crisis, emotionally bond with the opposite sex, take sides, etc. **Please follow this guideline.** We've also learned many things the hard way, and as a result you don't have to. We want to make sure that your own marriage does not suffer because of your willingness to help someone else.

- **It's always best to try to keep the meeting times to an hour (the first meeting may take longer) and to stick to the questions on the discussion sheets.** This will help you to avoid feeling overwhelmed by unnecessary details regarding marital problems and from the person possibly dishonoring their spouse in their sharing. It also protects and honors your time.

- **Remember that this program is first and foremost about helping the person get on track regarding their own life and walk with God.** We've found that reconciled marriages occur more as a result of changed hearts than fixed marriages. So, avoid "marriage counseling." Instead, help the person to focus on their own issues and activities rather than on what their spouse is or is not doing. Learn to gently bring him/her back to the questions, workbook lesson, and God's Word.

- **If the person's marriage status changes during the twelve-week period (one of them files for divorce, moves out, admits to a third party involvement, etc.) encourage the person you are supporting to continue as planned in the weekly meetings.** If the person you are supporting is the one responsible for the upheaval in the relationship, and they still agree to keep meeting with you, stand on God's Word (do not compromise what He says regarding sinful behavior), but continue to meet. You never know how God might use you and your commitment to convict and restore the individual.

- **If the person you are supporting backs away from the weekly commitment, there's nothing you can do. However, let them know that if they change their mind, you'll continue to meet.** If one of you must miss a week, then you can combine two weeks of lessons together at the next meeting, but try to be consistent regarding your meeting times.

# SUPPORT PARTNER GUIDELINES

- **Avoid discussing anything from your weekly meetings with their spouse or yours (again, we don't recommend your spouse meeting with theirs because of this problem).** The meetings should be treated very confidentially (see next paragraph). This will also help you avoid the he-said-she-said game. Couples in crisis have usually learned some manipulative tactics to "get messages" to each other. This only prolongs learning to communicate in a healthier way and puts you in the middle.

- **There might be situations when you will have to break a confidence.** If the person's life or someone else's life is in danger, seek outside intervention from local agencies and your pastor. It's always a good idea in your first meeting to say, "If you trust me enough to ask me to be your support partner, then consider trusting me if I find it necessary to get outside help.

- **Don't spend long telephone hours or daily contact with the person you are supporting.** Help and encourage him/her to create the support system we have recommended in the workbook and included below. This will help you to look forward to your meetings together, and will also help you to avoid burnout.

- **On your first meeting go over the section at the beginning of the Marriage 911: First Response Workbook on creating a support system.** Make sure they understand the importance of their support system. You will not be able to meet all of their needs, and a solid support system will help them through some potentially tough times. If a person does all the lessons and stays focused on God for the entire twelve-week period, you should begin to see a healthy shift occur from dependence on the support system to increased dependence on Christ for strength.

**Below we have included some excerpts from the workbook so you will know what the person you are supporting is being told and instructed to do.**

---

## BEFORE YOU BEGIN

**Materials needed:** Bible, journal or notebook, and your own copy of the workbook. It is also highly recommended that you read Yes, Your Marriage Can Be Saved, by Joe and Michelle Williams. This book will be a great supplement to the workbook, and will help you apply the concepts to your life in a more practical way.

**You will need a couple of days to establish your support system as you prepare to go through the workbook.** How you use the tools in the workbook, and how long it takes before you begin to experience major changes in your marriage, will depend on the following circumstances:

- *Whether or not your spouse is willing to participate.*
- *Whether you are separated or living together.*

- *Whether a third party, substance abuse, or physical abuse is involved .*
- *Your (and your spouse's) relationship with God.*
- *Your ability to meet regularly with your support person.*
- *Your sincere desire to reconcile.*
- *Your sincere desire to obey God.*

**The tools in this workbook can be used in whatever circumstance you are facing.** In the rare case where both you and your spouse want to reconcile at the same time, and both have a desire to obey God, the reconciliation process could take place very quickly. In those cases, we have witnessed marriages completely transformed within three months!

**Chances are, however, that you are beginning this workbook with one of you more willing than the other.** Some of you have a spouse who has no desire to even look at the workbook, and others of you may experience a willing spouse who becomes unwilling. Don't get discouraged. Joe and Michelle were off and on so often during their separation that it's a wonder they reconciled at all. Just remember that God is the God of miracles. While it's true that it takes two to reconcile a relationship, it only takes one of you to make the commitment to begin the process. **Let your spouse know that you are going through the material and give him/her information on how to purchase the workbook. Then don't mention it again, and pray! Let God do the rest. A lot can happen in three months, and this is your opportunity to do things God's way!**

## CREATE YOUR SUPPORT SYSTEM

**The most important thing you will do, after making the commitment to reconcile, is to put together your support system.** Without prayer and accountability you will not be strong enough to stand against the opposition of the enemy and bring harmony to your home. It will take supernatural power from God and the support of Christian friends.

**First, ask a Christian person (of your same gender) with a strong commitment to God and marriage if they would be willing to be your support person as you go through the workbook.** This would require meeting with them twelve times for one hour per week, in order to go over the discussion questions at the end of each chapter. We have found it to work best when the meetings are weekly to help you stay consistent and accountable. If you and your spouse are working through this program, your support partners should not be a married to each other. The reasons for this guideline is explained in the Marriage 911: First Response Support Partner Handbook. Your support person will need a copy of the Support Partner Handbook, which is available through our ministry if you did not receive one with this workbook.

**Next, prayerfully choose two or three Christian friends of your same gender who are supportive of your decision to have a good marriage and who will also help keep you accountable.** Friendships that will encourage you to honor your spouse in words and actions during this time, and who will pray for your marriage, will be very important. It may also mean that you will have to distance yourself from people who encourage the opposite. If you are separated, avoid singles groups and any social setting that could cause you to become "friends" with someone of the opposite sex. Separations that end in divorce often have a third party involved. List the names and numbers of supportive friends who come to mind:

## BE PREPARED

**You're about to begin a process that the enemy does not want to happen.** As long as Satan can divide families and keep homes broken, he has a better chance of destroying children and stopping the gospel of Christ from being spread. You are stepping into a battlefield, so be prepared. Read Ephesians 6:10-17, and plan on arranging your schedule to include the time that you'll need for prayer and workbook exercises.

---

*At this point as a support partner you might be asking yourself some "what if " questions. Here are a couple of common examples:*

- **What if the person you are supporting doesn't have anyone else to be in his or her support system?** Try to get them into a Bible Study of some kind or a same sex support group so that they can begin to meet others. Remind them that you cannot be their only "lifeline" during their crisis, even if they want you to be.

- **What if the person and their spouse are good friends of yours?** You must make a commitment to keep confidential what the individual shares with you. Do not discuss anything from your meeting times together with their spouse or yours or anyone else in your "friendship circle." If their marriage is in severe crisis (separation has occurred or is about to occur) you should limit contact as couples during the twelve-week period. You'll also need to take extra precautions to avoid hearing unnecessary details of marital conflicts so that you will not create an uncomfortable atmosphere between you after the reconciliation has taken place. If you don't feel you can do this, offer to be a part of their support system rather than the main support partner.

Regardless of your questions or apprehensions about being a support person, remember that God is the one in control. Through Him all things are possible (Matthew 19:26). Step out in faith and watch what He can do through you!

 If you have prayerfully accepted the opportunity to support someone whose marriage is in crisis, we would like to pray for you and assist you in any way. Your comments and experience as a support partner will help us in future workshops and teachings. We would like to ask you to visit the back of your resource at this time and ,all out a brief support partner form and send it to our team at NIM.

# CORE VALUES

As a support partner, we have some core values we would like for you to adopt to make this experience most successful.

At the National Institute of Marriage, there are several key principles that govern how we work with individuals and couples. Even with the most highly developed and best programs in the world, the results could still be ineffective if the people interacting with hurting people do not understand and hold some key values.

When our team works with couples, we make creating a safe environment a high priority. In short, we believe that people were created to live in the presence of the Lord, the safest place that exists. Unfortunately, in an unsafe environment, people abandon their posture of open, honest intimacy for a closed and protective posture. We believe an open and honest posture is our default setting and requires the least amount of energy to maintain. When people experience a safe environment over time, their hearts usually open to the point that they can receive the healing the Lord desires for all of us. We have listed a few of the key components of creating a safe environment.

• Respond with compassion. The main thing hurting people need to experience is loving people. Often times, people are hurting so badly that even believers feel that the Lord is a million miles away. Take this opportunity to allow them to experience the Lord's love through you.

• Feelings are neither right nor wrong, and therefore should not be judged. When a person is sharing their thoughts and feelings, please be careful not to judge them. Even if you feel you have biblical grounds to address an issue, please replace judgment with curiosity and allow the hurting person to better understand what is going on inside them. Judgment will hinder a person's willingness to openly disclose.

• You can't fix people; only the Lord can. Do not try to fix the problem for people. Walk with them as they discover truth.

• Use appropriate, vulnerable self-disclosure. Many times people feel a need to share from a place of expertise, and we feel this is very counterproductive. Instead, we recommend sharing your hurts and struggles in a "tastefully transparent" way (with limited details) to allow the hurting person to see you as a fellow life journeyer, and not as an "expert."

• Honor Walls. When someone determines that they do not want to discuss something, honor that. Stop and make sure they understand that you only want to discuss what they feel comfortable sharing. If they resist, please do not pressure them to share more.

 or  or

This program is designed for couples and individuals. If an individual has a spouse that is unwilling to participate this program will accommodate that need.

## First Response Team

The church is prepared with a lay based First Response Team prepared to meet with couples that are requesting help from the church. [The program can operate with as few as 2 First Responders]

 +  or  +  or

Following the 12 week program the couple meets with the First Response Team. The First Response Team member assesses the next step and makes recommendations to the participant(s).

Based on the amount of progress made in the 12 weeks of the program, the First Response Team Member makes recommendations for next steps.

- Any existing church resources, such as small groups, classes, bible studies etc.
- Referral to a trusted local Christian Counselor
- Referral to the National Institute of Marriage's Intensive Counseling Programs

x

 or  or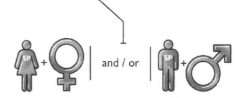

Members of the First Response team will meet with the individual or couple in crisis 1-2 times.

- Show compassion
- Introduce 1st Response Program and other relevant church and communication resources and services
- Encourage the participant(s) to select a support partner(s) or introduce a support partner(s) from the church if needed.
- Ask the participant(s) to commit to making no major decisions about their marriage for 12 weeks.

The participant(s) works through a 12 week program with a support partner that is chosen by the participant or assigned by the First Response Team. Husband and wife Support Partners should not work with the same participant couples. Wives should always have a female support partner and husbands should always have a male support partner.

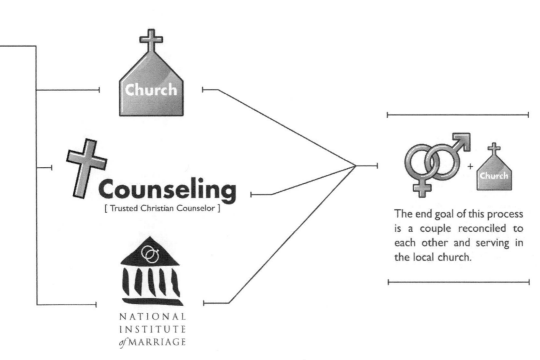

The end goal of this process is a couple reconciled to each other and serving in the local church.

# SUPPORT PARTNER QUESTIONNAIRE

*If you have prayerfully accepted the opportunity to support someone whose marriage is in crisis, we would like to pray for you and assist you in any way. Your comments and experience as a support partner will help us in future workshops and teachings. Thank you for taking the time to complete the following information and for contacting us if you have questions. (You may email us your comments and experience, or questions at: Info@Marriage911Godsway. com, or mail this page with your comments on the back at: Marriage 911 God's Way, 2132B Wylie Drive, Modesto, CA.)*

Date: _____

Name:

First _____    Last _____

Address: _____

City: _____    State: _____    Zip: _____

Phone: (_____) _____

Marital Status: _____ Church Affiliation:_____

Member?  Yes No


Thank You.  WWW.Marriage911Godsway.com

# WHERE'S YOUR FOCUS?

*Your marriage crisis is more about you and God than it is about you and your spouse.*

"Set your minds on things above, not on earthly things"(Colossians 3:2).

# WEEK ONE

## Unmet Needs

*Do you expect your spouse to meet all your needs?*

    This chapter deals with each person taking responsibility for meeting many of their own needs and to get their focus off their spouse to meet all their needs. We believe that it is impossible to

    expect another human being to be perfect enough to meet all your needs, but it is reasonable to want your needs to be satisfied. Between you and God, there are a host of righteous and empowering ways for this to be accomplished. We ask them to make a list of 15 or so activities that they can do alone, that are not immoral, illegal, or expensive (such as walking, biking, fishing, movies, window shopping, listening to music, etc.).

Reconciliation Tool — 1A
"The Three-Month Crisis Plan"

    We asked the person you are supporting to read a chapter in Proverbs each day while doing the workbook, and to communicate with God daily through journaling.

Reconciliation Tool 1B
"The Self-Nurture List"

    We asked the person you are supporting to make a list of 10-20 activities that they enjoy doing alone, and to choose one that is not immoral, illegal, or expensive. We ask them to begin implementing at least half of the activities listed into their life each week. One thing we notice in couples whose marriages are in crisis (and it was true for us as well), is that they seem to have lost a sense of themselves as individuals. The stress of marriage troubles combined with everyday demands have obscured the simple enjoyments in life.

# WEEK ONE DISCUSSION QUESTIONS

**Listen to the answers that the person you are supporting has written. If time permits and you feel led, share your own answers as well.**

 **Open in prayer**

1. What are your hopes for going through the Marriage 911: First Response program?

2. How did you and your spouse meet? When you were dating your spouse what were the qualities that made you enjoy his/her company?

3. What expectations did you have about your spouse before you got married?

4. Did any of those qualities lead you to believe that he/she was going to be the man/woman of your dreams?

5. Explain your current relationship to God in comparison to how it's been in the past.

6. What was one thing that God showed you in your study of Proverbs this week?

7. What "self-nurture activities" did you do this week? If none, what is your reason?

8. Share any additional thoughts, insights from the Lord, or experiences that have happened this week that challenged your thinking or impacted your heart.

9. What is one specific concern for which you would like prayer this week?

 **Close in prayer**

# NOTES

# WEEK TWO

## Selfless Behavior

*Are you trying to play God by trying to meet all your spouse's needs?*

Many people believe their ability to make someone happy makes them more loveable or more valuable, and as a result will lead to them being loved. Being needed can certainly be affirming. In the beginning of this type of a relationship both parties are usually thrilled with this set-up. But if the happiness of one's spouse becomes the focus of life as an attempt to secure love, it can be just as self- centered as the person who expects their spouse to meet all of his/her needs. In either case, the focus  is off God, and He considers this idolatry (see Exodus 20: 1-6). Sadly, this misguided focus not only distracts you and your spouse from God, but it also leads to feelings of resentment. At some point it becomes clear that no matter what you do, it will never be enough to secure happiness.

**From Michelle***: When I met Joe I was just getting over the pain of a divorce. I desperately wanted to give my love and affection to someone and to feel needed. I felt loved by Joe, and I enjoyed that I was able to make him happy. After we married, and reality set in, I felt smothered and controlled by his unrealistic expectations for me to meet all his needs.*

### Reconciliation Tool 2A
### "Encourage Your Spouse"

1.  In this tool, we asked the person you are supporting to ask his or her spouse (assuming they are still living together, or spending time together) to recall activities that he or she used to enjoy doing, but are not doing anymore, and to encourage their spouse to start doing those things again.

2.  If they are separated, we asked them to write a note apologizing for their part in having their spouse give up the hobbies/activities they once enjoyed and to encourage their spouse to take them up again (assuming those activities/hobbies are not immoral, illegal, or too expensive).

We tell them: "Sincerely ask God to reveal any role you may have played in your spouse giving up this activity. As you gain clarity, apologize and ask for their forgiveness.

You may find writing a note a bit stretching, especially if you feel that your spouse is self-centered and demanding, or if you are unsure of your spouse's response to the note. If you feel that you can verbally communicate to your spouse easier, then do that, but don't neglect this exercise; we have found that with this tool most couples have been able to begin the process of rebuilding mutual respect for one another and let go of some resentment. Later, as the tension eases between the two of you, and you both are willing, you can combine your lists and choose activities that the two of you can do together   as well. Some of the best conversations a couple can have often take place when you are sharing activities together.

# WEEK TWO DISCUSSION QUESTIONS

**Listen to the answers that the person you are supporting has written. If time permits and you feel led, share your own answers as well.**

 **Open in prayer**

1. Which has been more of a struggle for you: trying to be "the" source of your spouse's happiness or making your spouse "the" source of your happiness? Please explain.

2. In looking at it now, how productive has your approach been? How has it left you feeling about your spouse and your marriage? How has your approach left you feeling about you?

3. Did you write your spouse a note of encouragement? If not, why? If so, what response, if any, did you receive?

4. Did God reveal to you any part you may have played in your spouse giving up an enjoyed activity? Please describe.

5. What was one thing that God showed you in your study of Proverbs this week?

6. What "nurture activities" did you do this week? Did you and your spouse discuss any activities that you could begin doing again?

7. How well have you done in establishing a support network? Explain.

8. Share any additional thoughts, insights from the Lord, or experiences that have happened this week that challenged your thinking or impacted your heart.

9. Share one thing for which you are thankful and one concern.

 **Close in prayer.**

# NOTES

# WEEK THREE

## Caring for Self

*Are you exhausted and feeling hopeless?*

This chapter begins focusing on the person's relationship with God. We encourage him/her to become a member of a Bible-teaching church, if they are not in one already. We discuss the importance of understanding God's Word if they expect to know how to live life God's way, and ask that they carve a day out of their week to spend time with God. We give them an outline to follow for morning, early afternoon, and late afternoon.

Another tool we give in this chapter is our "Spiritual Fuel Tank Indicator." We have included a copy of that for you below.

### Reconciliation Tool 3A
### "Spend a Day with God"

In this tool, we give instruction on how to spend their day with God, with recommendations of a morning, afternoon, and evening schedule of prayer and Bible study.

### Reconciliation Tool 3B
### "The Spiritual Fuel Tank Indicator"

We explained to the person you are supporting:

When circumstances become stressful and feelings of uneasiness come over you, what is your first response? If you're like most, you'll probably do whatever you can to create peace in your life. That may be a good desire, but without a right relationship with God, the desire for peace can actually end up causing sinful behavior with results that end in anything but peace. Below is a tool that can help keep you focused in the right direction when you feel the first signs of uneasiness. Study the "spiritual fuel tank indicator" and notice that if you move the gauge arrow to the left of *uneasiness*, you will move into *self-will*, then into *ungodly acts* and eventually on "*E*," as you've eased God out of the situation. However, if you choose *prayer* at the first signs of uneasiness you will engage the supernatural power of God to give you the wisdom to discern any conviction the Holy Spirit wants to reveal to you, and eventually into "*F*," as you become full of God's love. As you practice consistently to focus on God and go to prayer when things are stressful, it will become a habit and you will be able to make wise decisions in all areas of your life.

[spiritual fuel tank indicator]

# WEEK THREE DISCUSSION QUESTIONS

**If the person you are supporting was unable to spend a day with God, discuss questions 5-9 and encourage him/her do make an effort to do so as soon as possible. We've seen people make a complete turn around in their thinking with this exercise.**

 **Open in prayer**

1. Describe any significant experiences or thoughts you had on your date with God.

2. How do you typically respond when you experience what feels like "God's silence" or an "unanswered prayer request?"

3. Were you able to reconcile with anyone whom God brought to your mind this week? How did you feel about asking that person for forgiveness, and how did they respond?

4. Were you able to identify some areas in your life that are out of balance, and, if so, how do you plan to become more balanced?

5. Are there some areas that are out of balance in your life over which you have very little control? What are they?

6. What is your impression of the focus meter? Where do you usually get stuck?

7. What has God shown you in His Word this week (Proverbs or other)?

8. Share any additional thoughts, insights from the Lord, or experiences that have happened this week that challenged your thinking or impacted your heart.

9. What is one thing that you are thankful for, and what is one concern to pray about.

 **Close in prayer**

# NOTES

# WEEK FOUR

## Valuing Differences
*Do you want the freedom to be who you are?*

We begin this chapter with an excerpt from Joe and Michelle, and their ongoing frustration with one another in the early days of their relationship. We quote Michelle as saying, *"Joe was determined to put fun into our marriage and I was goal-driven and wanted us to accomplish things. Then, one Sunday we happened to see some tapes on the different temperament styles, and it changed our marriage and home life forever."*

Joe and Michelle finally understood that neither was wrong. God actually designed them with their own temperament styles and with unique differences. After taking a temperament test, they began to understand each other's strengths and weaknesses. They were able to see each other in a whole new light and began to actually appreciate their God given differences. In fact, it brought so much new joy to their marriage because they realized that they really weren't trying to irritate each other. Rather, they were just wired differently.

In this chapter we go over the four basic temperaments: The Expressives ( "otter" or outgoing, "fun" personality), the Drivers (the "lion" or strong leader type), the Analyticals (the "beaver" or detailed perfectionist), and the Amiables (the "golden retriever" or the peacemaker). We have included the test for you to take as well, even if you have taken one in the past. It is important that the person you are supporting understand that this is just a tool and is not meant to put him/her in a box with a label. Help the person to focus on the strengths of their temperament (or combination of the two strongest).

**Reconciliation Tool 4A**
**"Focus On Your Mate's Good Qualities"**

**We asked the person you are supporting to get a package of 3x5 cards and for the next 8 weeks plan on using one card daily.** On your card each day (preferably during your daily quiet time) make a list of all the qualities that are positive in your spouse. If you have to remember back to your dating days, that's okay. If your spouse did something kind for you or one of your children, write it down. If they paid a bill, worked on your car, kept a commitment, or just said a kind word, make a note of it.

Jot down anything at all that comes to mind regarding the good qualities in your mate. Remember that everyone has strengths and weaknesses, and it's impossible for anyone not to have some good qualities. It is possible, however, for people to miss the good qualities because of focusing on the negative all the time.

You may find this exercise difficult to do for a couple of reasons. (I) You have probably not been used to thinking of your mate's good qualities because of past and present hurts, and (2) If you don't like to write, it will take discipline to write daily. But, this exercise is a very important part of the reconciliation process because it takes practice to get into the habit of changing the way you think about your spouse. If you write these positive traits down regularly, you will begin to change your thinking, and subsequently change your behavior toward your spouse. If you want to reconcile God's way, He commands that you love one another and not harbor bitterness. No matter how your spouse is behaving at the present time, do this exercise with all the determination you can muster. Trust God to give you the insight you need to focus on the positive!

### Reconciliation Tool 4B
### "Verbally Compliment Your Mate"

**We encouraged the person you are supporting to put joy back in his or her marriage by complimenting his or her spouse. We said**: Even in situations where couples are separated we have seen miracles happen just because the conversation between them changed from negative comments to positive ones. This last exercise in the Focus section of the workbook is one of the most important tools you will use in reconciling. Family members and friends need to hear you saying kind things about the person you are married to, not to mention that your spouse needs to hear it. This tool is for the benefit of everyone with whom you come in contact, including your spouse.

Make it a point to verbally compliment your spouse to his/her face or to someone else at least twice a day. Researchers have said that it takes five positive comments to erase one negative one, so if you really want to make a difference, do more. The habit of speaking positively about and to one another will be very important as we move into the next section of the workbook, and you continue to work on reconciling.

### TEMPERAMENT PROFILE
### Reconciling God's Way Ministries

*After studying the four choices across, please circle the word or sentence that best or most often describes you. You will probably identify with all to a degree, but circle only the one that best applies. If you are not sure, ask someone who knows you well.*

### Strengths

| | | | | |
|---|---|---|---|---|
| 1. | Full of life | Risk taker | Analytical | Adapts to any situation |
| 2. | Playful | Convincing | Finishes projects | Easy-going |
| 3. | Social | Head-strong | Self-sacrificing | Accepts others rules |
| 4. | Funny | Commanding | Reliable | Friendly |
| 5. | Cheerful | Self-assured | Artistic | Even-tempered |
| 6. | Talkative | Goal-oriented | Thoughtful | Tolerant |

| 7. | Lively | Leader | Loyal | Good listener |
|---|---|---|---|---|
| 8. | Inspiring | Independent | Expects perfection | Agreeable |
| 9. | Optimistic | Outspoken | Organized | Accommodating |

Subtotal your scores by adding the amount of each column, and go on to the next page.

## Weaknesses

| 10. | Undisciplined | Unsympathetic | Holds grudges | Lazy |
|---|---|---|---|---|
| 11. | Interrupts | Impatient | Never good enough | Indecisive |
| 12. | Too talkative | Inconsiderate | Easily offended | Peace at any cost |
| 13. | Naive | Overly confident | Negative | Unconcerned |
| 14. | Disorganized | Controlling | Depressed | Lack of confidence |
| 15. | Messy | Shrewd | Moody | Mumbles |
| 16. | Loud | Domineering | Avoids people | Too tired to work |
| 17. | Short attention span | Critical/judgmental | Manipulative | Too compromising |
| 18. | Inconsistent | Intolerant | Introvert | Indifferent |

_____  _____  _____  _____

Strengths (from previous page).

_____  _____  _____  _____

Grand totals

_____  _____  _____  _____

Developed By **Reconciling God's Way** Ministries

## Temperament Types
## Answer Sheet

After you have totaled all your answers, the column with the highest number will identify your temperament. The descriptions below are a summary of each temperament.

**Column One:** *Expressives* (Otter or Sanguine)

This personality type lives life to the fullest. They are carefree, and love to bring life and laughter to any group setting. People are usually drawn to their optimistic attitude and to their exuberant energy. The "Expressives" like to be involved in many things, and are very comfortable being the center of attention. Lack of discipline and organization can be a downfall to this type, especially if they work or live in an environment where organization and discipline are valued by others.

**Column Two:** *Drivers* (Lion or Choleric)

This personality type loves a challenge. They are natural leaders, and are very strong personality types. They are goal-oriented and driven toward success. They are self-assured and convincing, and people follow them. The "Drivers" have to be careful not to run over other people's thoughts and feelings. Insensitivity can be a downfall.

**Column Three:** *Analyticals* (Beaver or Melancholy)

This is the perfectionist type. The "Analyticals" are detail-oriented and organized. They work hard at doing things right. The Analyticals also tend to be black and white thinkers (things are right or wrong, with very little grey). They have high standards for themselves, but need to be careful not to impose those standards on others. Their weakness might be in the area of being critical or judgmental.

**Column Four:** *Amiables* (Golden Retriever or Phlegmatic)

This is the peacemaker personality type. The Amiables don't like conflict and err on the side of "peace at any cost." They are warm, friendly and caring people whom others enjoy being around. Their downside is usually in the area of laziness, or losing who they are in order to please others.

Remember that God created us in His image, and that Jesus' personality was perfectly balanced. While we are not (and never will be) perfect, we are to strive for a healthy balance in our behavior.

Read the strengths of the temperaments in which you scored low, and stretch yourself whenever possible to implement some of those strengths in your life. Look over the strengths of yourself and your mate, and try as often as you can to be thankful for those strengths, and use them for the glory of God!

*If you are interested in a very detailed and fascinating personality profile, go to national marriage. com, and order the Enneagram personality test. After completing the test on the cd, you will receive a 5-9 page detailed report on your personality type. It is also interesting to read the interactive reports to understand how your personality type and that of your spouse interact together.

# WEEK FOUR DISCUSSION QUESTIONS

**Listen to the answers that the person you are supporting has written. If time permits and you feel led, share your own answers as well.**

 **Open in prayer**

1. What are your two strongest temperaments/traits?

2. What are the strongest temperaments/traits in the rest of your family (and spouse)?

3. What strengths do you exhibit most frequently? What about your spouse?

4. What weaknesses do you struggle with most?

5. Were you able to verbally compliment your spouse? Were you able to compliment someone else?

6. What has God shown you this week in your study of Proverbs?

7. Share any additional thoughts, insights from the Lord, or experiences that have happened this week that challenged your thinking or impacted your heart.

8. What is one thing you are thankful for this week? What concern can your support partner pray for this week?

 **Close in prayer**

# NOTES

# WHERE'S YOUR HEART?

*The secrets in your heart are powerful predictors of present and future pain.*

"Search me, 0 God, and know my heart; test me and know my anxious thoughts"(Psalm 139:23).

# WEEK FIVE

## Secret Motives
*Do you really want to reconcile?*

When actors are on stage rehearsing their lines for a play, oftentimes the director will walk by and call out *"subtext."* The director wants to know from the actors if they understand the underlying theme of the play and if they really know the meaning of their lines. For instance, if the actors are supposed to be in love, their body language and the way they deliver their lines should show that. The audience would be confused if the lines were delivered in a tone of voice and body movements that contradicted the subtext (or subplot) of the play.

### Reconciliation Tool 5A
### "Ask Tough Questions"

**In this exercise, we asked the person you are supporting to sincerely think through any ulterior motives they may have for going through this workbook. This exercise is very important. We tell them:** Depending on how long your relationship has been stressed, you have both been living in a situation that is difficult. In stressful situations it's tempting to want to be free from the pain, even if it means going against God's Word. Pray before you begin this exercise and answer the following questions:

1. List 5-10 reasons why you want your marriage to stay together:


2. List any reason at all that comes to mind as to why you might be afraid to stay with your spouse (this would include any immoral behavior going on either on your behalf or your spouse's, i.e., adultery, drugs or alcohol, abuse of you or children, pornography, etc.) Please be honest in this section. If you are concerned about writing in this workbook, write in code that only you would understand, or use a separate sheet of paper and throw it away after this exercise is completed. If your spouse is involved in any immoral behavior and refuses to repent, you will need to address that separately. A pastor or Christian counselor who is skilled in how to set up healthy relationship boundaries can help guide you.

*(Ask the person you are supporting to share any answers they feel comfortable sharing with you).*


3. In what ways have you sent mixed or confusing messages to your spouse about your intent to reconcile?

# WEEK FIVE DISCUSSION QUESTIONS

**Listen to the answers that the person you are supporting has written. If time permits and you feel led, share your own answers as well.**

 **Open in prayer**

1. Share your answer to Reconciliation Tool 5A. What are the reasons you want to reconcile?

2. Share your answers as to what you fear about reconciling?

3. If the Holy Spirit convicted you this past week in a particular area, please share it with your support partner. It will be important for you to bring it to light and make a commitment to be held accountable for the remainder of your time together.

4. Share your answers from the Scriptures that you studied this week. Which one was most meaningful?

5. In your study of Proverbs this week, what did God show you?

6 Share any additional thoughts, insights from the Lord, or experiences that have happened this week that challenged your thinking or impacted your heart.

7. Share with your support partner one thing that you are thankful for and one concern for which you need prayer.

 **Close in prayer.**

# NOTES

# WEEK SIX

## Secret Anger

*Understand your anger....revolutionize your marriage!*

This chapter deals with the issue of anger. Anger and honesty are two areas that we have found in our years of helping others (as well as in our own marriage) that couples seem to struggle with the most. In this week's lesson, we identify the most common responses to the emotion of anger, and we give the person you are supporting an opportunity to identify their most commonly used expression. We have included the page for you that list the four different types of expressions. We explain that the basic reasons people feel angry are: hurt, frustration, fear and injustice. We ask the person you are supporting to track which area they experience most often by keeping a record for the week of every time they feel angry.

### Reconciliation Tool 6A
### "Identify Your Choice Of Expression"

**According to Neil Clark Warren {author of *Make Anger Your Ally*) there are four main techniques with which people identify.** Listed below are the four techniques (the terms are taken from Neil's book). Rate them in order of #I-4, with #I being the technique you choose most. Then, next to your rating, put your spouse's. Notice that they are all negative responses. We'll give you some tools for positive responses later on.

Rate _____

1. **Exploder:** People who explode never have ulcers (but everyone around them does!) Exploders use their aggressive behavior (yelling, slamming things, physical altercations, etc.) to intimidate and control others.

Rate _____

2. **Somatizer:** This person pretends that everything is fine when it isn't. They don't look angry, but inside they are in knots. They have headaches, colitis, stomach problems and unidentified illnesses. Possibly the only time they ever got attention as children was when they were ill.

Rate _____

3. **Self-Punisher:** This person has turned his/her anger in on themselves. They are usually perfectionists, and because they aren't "perfect" they become frustrated. Consequently, most of them struggle with depression. Sadness, withdrawal and self-blame are ongoing in their lives.

# WEEK SIX - SECRET ANGER

Rate _____

4.  **Underhandler:** Judas was an underhandler in his dealings with Jesus and the disciples. This person pretends to be your friend, but in reality is coming in through the back door as your enemy. They don't have many close friends and are gossips and backbiters. They also tend to be passive-aggressive. It is suggested that people who choose to express their anger in this method were not allowed to show any anger expression at home while growing up.

### Reconciliation Tool 6B
### "Identify Your Anger"

We asked the person you are supporting to:"Get a couple of 3x5 cards, (or small note pad) and carry them with you this whole week. Every time you feel the emotion of anger, and you start to express it by one of the four choices, jot it down. Write whether you were **frustrated**, **fearful**, **hurt** (emotionally or physically), or experienced an **injustice** (yourself or someone else's).And yes, you can experience a couple or even all four at once. This is an important step because you will begin to see a pattern for what makes you angry, and that will come in handy in the next step."

### Reconciliation Tool 6C
### "Bring It to the Light"

This is where the importance of being honest and not fearing others more than God comes in. Being honest with what you are feeling, and being real with your spouse, will help you to bring anger issues to the light and not let Satan have a foothold (*Ephesians 4: 27*). This last tool this week will take much practice, so don't get discouraged. Your assignment is to just grasp the concept, and practice it as much as you possibly can.

1.  **The next time you feel anger, say so out loud and identify exactly why you are angry.** For instance, if you are frustrated because you can't find something and it's causing you to be late for an appointment, say, 'I'm really frustrated right now because I can't find (my keys) and it's making me late."

2.  **Then, after identifying your reason aloud, pray aloud for God to give you supernatural strength and wisdom not to sin in your frustration (anger).** If it's another person triggering your frustration, identify out loud to the person that you are feeling frustrated (they know it anyway), but do not use the word "angry"—keep it to the issue of "frustration," (or fear, injustice, or hurt).This is crucial for learning to express anger without sinning, and it truly will bring a new respect to you and others once it's learned. The reason for not using the word "anger" in dealing with the other person is because the word itself is so vague and so often used negatively, that they become defensive as soon as they hear it. But the words "fear", "frustration", "hurt", and "injustice" are emotions with which people can more easily identify thus diffusing any defensive reactions more quickly, depending on the emotional maturity of the other person.

If it's inappropriate to pray aloud in the moment, God can hear your silent plea to Him and He will give you the strength and wisdom not to sin in your anger. But you must ask and believe (see *James 1: 5-6)*.

3. **The final step in this last tool is to confess your own contribution to the situation.** If there is anything you need to confess, do it. Once you ask God to give you the wisdom you need, He will show you your part in the situation. It is important that you not get into the habit of thinking that every situation that causes you to feel angry is always someone else's fault.

# WEEK SIX DISCUSSION QUESTIONS

**Listen to the answers that the person you are supporting has written. If time permits and you feel led, share your own answers as well.**

 **Open in prayer**

1.  After reading about the different ways people express anger, how did you rate yourself?

2.  Did you track what made you angry this week? If not, why? If so, do you want to share a couple of situations with your support partner?

3.  Did you tell anyone this week that you were frustrated, fearful, hurt, or felt an injustice? If so, explain how it took place and what happened afterwards.

4.  What did God show you this week concerning Proverbs?

5.  Share any additional thoughts, insights from the Lord, or experiences that have happened this week that have challenged your thinking or impacted your heart.

6.  Tell your support partner one thing he/she can be in prayer for this week, and give one praise report. You have made it half way through the workbook. As you close in prayer this week, ask God to help you complete your commitment.

 **Close in prayer**

# NOTES

## Secret Lies

*Honesty is at the core of true intimacy.*

This chapter deals with the area of honesty in the marriage. In order for there to be true intimacy (in-to-me-see), there must be truth and transparency. There are four main reasons people are dishonest: to protect others, to avoid trouble, chronic lying (habitually, for no apparent reason), and for control. We ask the person to rank the reasons he/she tends to be dishonest with #I being the primary one and #4 being the least. The Scriptures we ask them look up and rewrite in their own words are: *Ephesians 4:25, Colossians 3:9-10, Proverbs 14:5, and 12:22, Romans 16: 17-19, and 1 Corinthians 13:4-7.*

**Reconciliation Tool 7A**
**"Take the Risk"**

We challenged the person you are supporting to identify the reasons they might not be totally honest with their mate. This isn't just about telling lies, it's about withholding information, twisting facts, and manipulating circumstances as well.

In this tool, we said:

1.  **Identify which area you tend to struggle with the most when it comes to being dishonest, and rate them in order (mark 1 for the one you struggle with the most and 4 for the one you struggle with the least).**

**Protecting** (you want to keep others from suffering consequences or pain)

Rate _____

**Avoiding trouble** (you fear others' reactions or rejection)

Rate _____

**Chronic lying** (you exaggerate or lie for no reason)

Rate _____

**Controlling** (you manipulate to get your way)

Rate _____

I. We said: **Ask God to give you the supernatural strength you will need in order to obey Him the next time you are faced with having to be honest in a situation that you'd rather be dishonest in.**

2.   **Then, look for an opportunity to practice taking the risk to be honest with your mate or anyone else that God puts in your path.** Once you decide to start practicing truth instead of dishonesty, you'll probably start seeing many areas in your life that you've not been honest in and had not even realized it. These days, "situational ethics" and being politically correct are so much a part of our world that it's getting harder all the time to recognize dishonesty for what it is.

**Reconciliation Tool 7B
"What Does God Say?"**

In this tool, we said:

**Look up the following Scriptures and write in your own words what those Scripture verses say to you about the importance of honesty.**

*Ephesians 4:25*

*Colossians 3:9-10*

*Proverbs 14:5*

*Proverbs 12:22*

*Romans 16:17-19*

I Corinthians 13:4-7

**Listen to the answers that the person you are supporting has written. If time permits and you feel led, share your own answers as well.**

 **Open in prayer**

1. Share how you rated yourself on the dishonesty scale. Explain your answer.

2. Did you always struggle with dishonesty in that way prior to marriage? If so, describe how this played out in other relationships or in childhood.

3. Did you have an opportunity this week to speak truth when you could have been dishonest? Please explain.

4. In your exercise this week on looking up verses in tool 7B, was there a verse that stood out to you on the issue of honesty?

5. Do you find that you tend to be fearful that your mate is not always being honest? List some reasons that tend to make you fearful of being honest in all circumstances (this will be helpful for next week too):

6. What was one thing that God showed you in your study of Proverbs this week?

7. Share any additional thoughts, insights from the Lord, or experiences that have happened this week that challenged your thinking or impacted your heart.

8. Have you been able to continue doing your nurture activities weekly? If not, what has prevented you from doing so?

9. Share with your support partner one thing that you are thankful for and one concern for him/her to pray about for you.

 **Close in prayer.**

# NOTES

## Secret Fears

*What keeps you from being real with your mate?*

This chapter helps the person face some of the fears they may be having in the marriage. Some are imagined and some are real. It will be important for you to watch for signs in the marriage that might be posing physical dangers or severe emotional abuse. In this week's lesson we have listed for them the most common fears in marriage, and we ask that the person put a check mark on each one that is relevant in their own marriage. There are five marked with "*", which deal with spousal abuse, children's safety, and suicide. If the person you are supporting has marked any of those, it will be important for you to help him/ her contact the proper agency in order to get the help needed. Please do not try to deal with these issues on your own unless you are a professional counselor or pastor. **This is the time to get outside help as we mentioned in the beginning of this handbook**. Most agencies are listed in the front of your telephone book. You should encourage the person to meet with their pastor as well. The Scriptures we ask the person to personalize are: *James I:5* and *Luke I2:II*.

### Reconciliation Tool 8A
### "Identify Your Fears"

*A list of fears is given for them to identify which ones they experience, and indicate how strong the fear is).*

### Reconciliation Tool 8B
### "Identify Dangerous Situations"

*(Some of the fears that are listed imply dangerous situations, and a proactive response is listed for them to follow if they find themselves in such danger.)*

4.   **Last, do not let your fear stop you from doing what you need to do.** If your marriage has any hope at all, it will be because you have not allowed fear to control your response to your spouse's behavior.

### Reconciliation Tool 8C
### "When Afraid, Rely on God"

*(Verses are given for them to personalize)*

**Listen to the answers that the person you are supporting has written. If time permits and you feel led, share your own answers as well.**

 **Open in prayer**

1. Look at what you wrote on tools 8A and 8B. Share with your support person any of the #2's or #3's that you feel comfortable discussing. (If you checked any questions marked with *, make certain you let them know if you have contacted your pastor or anyone else for help or referral. Please do not ask them to keep information like that to themselves and not involve outside help. It puts them in an unfair and compromising situation.)

2. Was there an opportunity this week to be vulnerable with your mate in an area that has normally been difficult? How about with someone else?

3. Is there anyone in your life at this time (besides possibly your spouse) whose reactions you fear? If so, how do you intend to begin changing the way you respond to their negative behavior? (Discuss the Scriptures you personalized.)

4. What did you relate to in Proverbs this week?

5. Share any additional thoughts, insights from the Lord, or experiences that have happened this week that challenged your thinking or impacted your heart.

6. What praise report and prayer concern do you have for this week?

 **Close in prayer.**

# NOTES

# WHERE'S YOUR HOPE?

*It is not you who is able to reconcile, by Christ is you!*

"…for it is God who works in you to will and to act according to His good purpose"(Philippians 2:13).

# WEEK NINE

## Know How To Recognize Hope

*Bad habits are hard to break.*

This chapter deals with bad habits, and the importance of learning to be *proactive* rather than *reactive*. We ask the person to put him/herself in a stressful situation and decide beforehand that he/she will be able to get through it with a godly attitude. It will be important for the person to be studying the Scripture verses we have recommended as they prepare to move into the final section of the workbook, "Where is Your Hope?" Of course the person's hope is found only in Jesus, and this will be an opportunity for you to share more about God's love. Depending on your knowledge of the Bible, and what kind of relationship you have been able to build (or may have already had) with the person you are supporting, you can begin introducing them into more of what God's Word has to say about how to live life even in the midst of stressful circumstances. We also ask the person to go back and begin doing any of the exercises he/she might have missed or stopped doing. Gently confront the person if you see a slacking off in finishing the lessons. This section is very important, and obviously your commitment in doing your part will be necessary as well. The Scriptures that we ask the person to look up and complete are: *Romans 15:5-7, Romans 8:8-9, and 1Peter 1:13-16. We also discuss faith (Matthew 17:20).*

### Reconciliation Tool 9A
### "Recognize Where Your Hope Is"

(Verses are given for them to look up and personalize as a way to stay focused on God.)

### Reconciliation Tool 9B
### "Practice Being Proactive"

We explain that one of the best ways to become disciplined and learn self-control, is to allow yourself to be put in situations that are stressful and that would normally cause you to be reactive rather than proactive. By choosing to be in the situation, you can also choose how you will respond. Then when similar situations arise you can be better prepared. We encourage them to choose to put themselves in stressful situations (i.e. go to the slowest line in the grocery store) to practice patience and self-control.

# WEEK NINE DISCUSSION QUESTIONS

**Listen to the answers that the person you are supporting has written. If time permits and you feel led, share your own answers as well.**

 **Open in prayer**

1.  When you and your spouse disagree on something, what is a typical argument like? Are you silent, talkative, pouty, shouty, etc.?

2.  What habits do you have that you wish you didn't? Were you able to begin working on any of them this week? If not, why?

3.  Do you tend to be reactive rather than proactive?

4.  Did you have an opportunity to practice any of the situations this week that would help build your self-control? If so, share the experience. If not, do you plan to, and if so, which example?

5.  Of the Scriptures that you looked up this week, which one spoke to you the most?

6.  Were you able to ask a relative close to you (or your spouse) to share one area that you should work on? How did it go?

7.  What proverb meant the most to you this week? (Also see Proverbs 17:27-28.)

8.  Share any additional thoughts, insights from the Lord, or experiences that have happened this week that challenged your way of thinking or impacted your heart.

9.  What is a praise that you have for the week? What is a prayer request?

 **Close in prayer.**

# NOTES

# WEEK TEN

## Know What To Avoid
*God's timing is not always ours.*

This chapter focuses on God's timing and six things to avoid when waiting on God: (I) Being overly confident; (2) Leads to Confusion; (3) Too many counselors; (4) Playing God by rescuing; (5) Being paralyzed by fear; and (6) Comparing to others. Trusting God while waiting for His direction is something we all struggle with, and in a stressful marriage it's going to be especially difficult. The Scriptures we ask the person to write out and personalize are: *I Corinthians 14:33, Philippians 4:5-7, Psalm 116:1-3, Matthew 11:29-30, Proverbs 19:19, Hebrews 12:11, 2 Timothy 1:7, Matthew 10:26-27, Romans 12:3-5, and Galatians 5:24-26.*

### Reconciliation Tool 10A
### "Six Things to Avoid When Attempting to Follow God"

*(I. Avoid being overly confident. 2. Avoid making hasty decisions. 3. Avoid too many counselors. 4. Avoid rescuing and playing God. 5. Avoid being paralyzed by fear. 6. Avoid comparing your marriage with others)*

This list is explained and expounded upon in their workbook. Feel free to have the person you are supporting go over what these mean when they are with you.

# WEEK TEN DISCUSSION QUESTIONS

**Listen to the answers that the person you are supporting has written. If time permits and you feel led, share your own answers as well.**

 **Open in prayer**

1. Do you tend to have a hard time knowing if it is your will or God's will when you make a decision?

2. If you answered yes, what are some of the ways that you have made decisions in the past and God confirmed that they were His will?

3. Can you remember a time that you tried to do something on your own and God stopped you?

4. In your study of Scriptures this week, which ones were especially helpful?

5. Of the six principles we shared, which one related to you the most?

6. Which proverb spoke to you this week in your regular reading?

7. Share any additional thoughts, insights from the Lord, or experiences that have happened this week that challenged your thinking or impacted your heart.

8. What is a praise you have, and what is a prayer request for this week?

 **Close in prayer.**

# NOTES

# Know Who Is On Your Team

*Turn opposition into optimism.*

This chapter deals with the oppositions in life that causes all of us to deal with emotions such as: anxiety, envy, jealousy, bitterness, lust, and worry. We ask the person you are supporting to realize that there are only two options when dealing with oppositions in life: (I) Do things man's way (in the flesh) or (2) Do them God's way (in the spirit). We also explain the strength of a marriage relationship when the husband and wife join together to fight off opposition that comes in to destroy the family. We give 7 "Battle Strategies" to help the couple deal with a list of common oppositions that attack marriages. If the person you are supporting is going through the workbook with his or her spouse, then this lesson will be easier for him/her than someone going through it separated. Another factor is whether or not the person's spouse that you are supporting is an abuser (either mentally or physically). It will be important to go back and review week eight on fear, and reassess the marriage relationship again. If there are any areas that are still marked with "*" on their list of fears, then the person you are supporting was probably unable to do the exercise on page 72 of the workbook (#2 Join Forces With Your Spouse). If this is the case, make sure that the person is implementing the advice of the recommended agency and/or their pastor while they are completing the workbook. The Scriptures quoted for personalizing are: *Matthew 5:44, 1 Corinthians 6:9-10, 19-20, Ephesians 5:29, Romans 12:18, 1 Corinthians 10:13, Ephesians 5:19-20, 4:15-16, and 1 Peter 5:10.*

Discuss the entire chapter and Scriptures quoted, and pray with the person you are supporting, finding out where the direction of the marriage seems to be heading. Remember to point him/her back to Scripture, and let God work. Don't be discouraged if reconciliation hasn't been completed to both of your satisfactions. We have witnessed couples going through the workbook more than once while waiting for an answer to their marriage situation. (Use back of page for your notes.)

### Reconciliation Tool 11A
### "Rate Your Oppositions"

(A list of typical outside stressors is given to them. They are asked to rate the frequency in which they experience those outside oppositions).

### Reconciliation Tool 11B
### "Build Your Team"

(They are encouraged to build a support system with those who are encouraging their relationship, and are asked to meet with their spouse to ask for forgiveness, and to see if he/she might be interested in reconciliation).

**Reconciliation Tool 11C**
**"Seven Battle Strategies"**

(We offer a practical list of 7 strategies to implement when a person feels under attack.)

# WEEK ELEVEN DISCUSSION QUESTIONS

**Listen to the answers that the person you are supporting has written. If time permits and you feel led, share your own answers as well.**

 **Open in prayer**

I. Discuss what God has been saying to you through your scripture reading this past week.

2. Name all the categories you checked on Tool IIA. How do those outside stressors affect your marriage?

3. Did you have an opportunity to ask your spouse for forgiveness, and to see if he/she would consider reconciliation? If so, how did it go?

4. Have you had an opportunity to use the 7 battle strategies yet? If so, how did it go? If not, how useful do you feel those will be to you? Why?

5. Have you typically perceived your spouse more as your ally or your enemy throughout marriage?

6. What were the high points in your life this past week?

7. What were the low points in your life this past week?

8. What do you need prayer for as you face this coming week?

 **Close in prayer.**

# NOTES

# WEEK TWELVE

## Know When To "Go Forth"
*Whatever the outcome, use it for good.*

The last chapter of the workbook focuses on preparing the person you are supporting for how God will use this experience in their life to help others. Some will have reconciled, some will have actually separated during the twelve-week period, and some may still be in a holding pattern, waiting for the outcome of their situation. If the person you are supporting has been faithful in meeting, doing their lessons, and learning to focus on God instead of their mate, you will be blessed by seeing a changed person before your eyes-regardless of the outcome of their marriage so far! If he/she has not been faithful, and if the lessons were done half-heartedly, then you may only see dim flickers of hope. If that's the case, and you feel led by God to do so, ask them if they'd be willing to continue meeting for a while in order to go back through some of the lessons.

Read the last chapter and conclusion comments in the workbook together during your meeting time and discuss where the person you are supporting feels called. The Scriptures recommended for reading and writing out related to the tools below are: *Ephesians 6:10-20, I Corinthians 12:7-11, Proverbs 1:1-7, Isaiah 35:8, 46:10-11, 66:13, and Matthew 6:25-27.*The last paragraph is *Colossians 1:15-20* (written out) and focuses on the Person of Jesus in His relationship to God.

**Reconciliation Tool 12A**
**"Prepare For the Journey"**

**Reconciliation Tool 12B**
**"Trust God With The Outcome"**

**Reconciliation Tool 12C**
**"Know The Way"**

What if they need more help? (This is taken from the workbook so you will know what they were told, and how to encourage them.)

Hopefully you now have a solid support system in place and will continue to stay connected. We all need good counsel from time to time. However, if you are still feeling that you need more, that is not uncommon, weird, or weak. You are going through challenges that none of us are really prepared or trained to handle alone. If you are seeing a good counselor or pastor that is both supporting and prompting you forward, both personally and relationally, stay connected with him/her. If you are not currently working with a good counselor or pastor, find one. If you don't know of one, ask your church for a referral, or call at the National Institute of Marriage (417) 335-5882 and we'll help you find one.

If you would like more information about the National Institute of Marriage Intensive Programs (our Marriage Emergency Room) call us at the above number or go to our website at www.nationalmarriage. com. Our website is filled with lots of useful information, books, articles, and plenty to help you decide if an Intensive is for you, or introduce you to a variety of other available resources. If you do call us our consultants will be happy to answer any questions you might have. But whatever you decide to do, if you are struggling don't try to go it alone. Stay connected to God, and allow yourself to be supported by your brothers and sisters in Christ – your spiritual family.

# WEEK TWELVE DISCUSSION QUESTIONS

**We told the person you are supporting to: Please remember that it took longer than twelve weeks for your marriage to get into a crisis, so it may take longer than twelve weeks for you to realize full reconciliation in your marriage. The most important thing at this point is to stay focused on God and let Him continue to lead you into the plan He has for your life.**

**Listen to the answers that the person you are supporting has written. If time permits and you feel led, share your own answers as well.**

**Open in prayer**

1) Go through the verses and questions from tool 12B and 12C, and discuss the ones that impacted you in some way.

2) Of these past 12 chapters, what three things have surprised you the most?

3) What have you learned about yourself?

4) What have you learned about your spouse?

5) How has this experience impacted your faith?

6) How are you different today from how you were when you started this program?

**Now switch roles for a minute. Here are three questions for you to ask your support partner. (The person you are supporting will ask you these)**

7) Ask your support partner how this experience has impacted him/her over the past twelve weeks.

8) Ask your support partner if he/she was surprised by any changes that happened over the twelve weeks.

9) Ask your support partner to give you feedback on what he/she sees as next steps for you.

**Graciously thank your support partner for his/her investment in your life, and conclude in prayer together.**

# NOTES

# IN CONCLUSION

There are a few things to consider when your time together is up. One thing is that the person you have been supporting will need to continue studying God's Word. If you have realized that you have a lot in common, enjoy each other's company, and would even like to continue meeting but do not want to repeat the workbook, then consider going through an in-depth discipleship series together. There are a number of studies available at Christian bookstores, or through your church.

Another consideration would be to continue supporting the person, but not weekly. In that case, you might choose to meet monthly for the next few months, while the person moves into a different method of studying God's Word weekly.

In most cases, however, support partners help the person to move on to a Bible study, home church, or ministry opportunity, and make room in their schedule to begin supporting someone new. The most important thing is to make sure that you have a positive closure to your time together, and that you help the person get plugged in to other Christians studying God's Word.

We would appreciate you filling out the information on the following page in order for us to implement your feedback into our program. You can also go to nationalmarriage.com, and fill out this form on the Support Partner section of the "Marriage 911: A First Response" section. Your comments are important to us. Thank you for taking the time to do that.

God bless you for your commitment to serve as a support person. If you have comments, suggestions, success stories and/or praise to share, we would love to hear from you. Write the National Institute of Marriage, 250 Lakewood Dr., Hollister, MO 65672, or e-mail us at: nationalmarriage.com.

In His service,

All of us at the National Institute of Marriage
In partnership with Joe and Michelle Williams

Manufactured by Amazon.ca
Bolton, ON

18012678R00037